Tracks

Dr. Norma F. Lee

Copyright © 2012 Dr. Norma Lee

All rights reserved.

ISBN: **9798847734585**

DEDICATION

This particular copy of my book belongs to you, the reader. However, the inspiration for every copy belongs to:

My four Precious Blessings:

Norcha Miyah
Roshieck Latrell
William Ray, Jr.
Britiny Marie

and

My eleven Grandblessings:

Zan 'Juan William
Zharia Unea
Kyra Sharaven
Patrick Glen Jr.
Jason Jr.
Norman Latrell
Bryson Chandler
Lacee Grace
Micah James
Faith Marie
Jaxon Jerome

I am dedicating this book to my children and grandchildren because, unless the sun burns the earth in the next few years, this book will outlast me. I want something that will be around longer than I to show that there was once a **"GG"** who loved them with her whole heart and set them on their paths to everlasting life by ensuring they learned scriptures via Junior Bible Quiz (JBQ) and Teen Bible Quiz (TBQ). Also, I am passing on my motto to them, **"Don't quit, and never, never give up!!!"**

TABLE of CONTENTS

ACKNOWLEDGMENTS	i
Introduction	ii
1 CHRISTIAN'S DECLARATIONS	2
2 ENCOURAGEMENT FOR THE JOURNEY	7
3 POWER FILLED	31
4 GIFTS OF THE HOLY SPIRIT	34
5 MOUNT UP AS EAGLES	40
6 APPEAL TO PARENTS, GRANDPARENTS, AND FAMILIES	45
7 REWARDS AWAITING IN HEAVEN	46
8 CONCLUSION	50
REFERENCES	51
Bradley, M. (2021). Traits of the Eagle and How It Pertains To Our Christian Walk.	51
ABOUT THE AUTHOR	52

ACKNOWLEDGMENTS

First, I give honor to God, who is the head of my life and the Author and Finisher of my Faith, and I remain humble and grateful for all of the things He has done for me. He continues to amaze me as the spiritual anointing from the Holy Ghost tells me 1) what I need to do, 2) when I need to act, 3) directions I need to take, and 4) changes I need to make.

Deepest thanks go to my family for their support, advice, and perspectives. Also, the many hugs and smiles always cleared my mind and motivated me to continue writing.

To everyone who encouraged me along the way, whether in the community, at work, or at church, thank you so much! You continue to propel me to do bigger and better things. Deepest thanks to my patient, dedicated, and helpful editor, Kelly Wise. Kelly regularly communicated with me, keeping me abreast throughout the entire editing process.

Romans 10:14 cautions us, "...And how can they hear without someone preaching to them?" Thank you, Pastor Scott Holmes and Kara Featherston Holmes, for your continued service to the flock. Thank you for being truthful, fair, open, transparent, and not afraid to give honor to all – even children. It is apparent that your lives are devoted wholeheartedly to Jesus, both externally and internally. Keep pressing onward, Christian soldiers!

Introduction

"But as it is, they desire a better country, that is, a heavenly one. Therefore, God is not ashamed to be called their God, for he has prepared for them a city" **(Hebrews 11:16, ESV).**

Tracks to Heaven was the first book I wrote. In this sequel, *Tracks to Heaven 2*, I will continually refer to our eternal home. I am reminded of **Hebrews 13:14 (TLB)** where we are admonished, "For this world is not our home; we are looking forward to our everlasting home in heaven." *Tracks to Heaven 2* is designed to give a *preparation perspective.* As Christians, we will not just automatically go to Heaven; we must *prepare* for that beautiful city not made by the hands of man. Therefore, we do not prepare by attempting to earn our *salvation* but rather earn our *rewards* in Heaven.

John the revelator wrote, "I saw the Holy City, the new Jerusalem, coming down out of heaven from God, prepared as a bride beautifully dressed for her husband. And I heard a loud voice from the throne saying, 'Look! God's dwelling place is now among the people, and he will dwell with them. They will be his people, and God himself will be with them and be their God. He will wipe every tear from their eyes. There will be no more death or mourning or crying or pain, for the old order of things has passed away.' He who was seated on the throne said, 'I am making everything new!' Then he said, 'Write this down, for these words are trustworthy and true' " **(Revelation 21:2-5, NIV).**

John continues, "The angel who talked with me had a measuring rod of gold to measure the city, its gates and its walls" **(Revelation 21:15, NIV).** The city was laid out like a square, as long as it was wide. He measured the city with the rod and found it to be 12,000 stadia, a sports arena with tiers of seats for spectators in length, and as wide and high as it is long **(Revelation 21:16, NIV).**

Thus, we must perceive Heaven and prepare ourselves to stand before Christ one day. Then, as we stand before Christ, we will have two options – rewards or regrets! Enjoy reading *Tracks to Heaven 2* to get a *preparation perspective of that Holy City. So here is the question: Are you living with heaven in view?*

1 CHRISTIAN'S DECLARATIONS

Understanding who we are in Christ is absolutely essential for our success in this life as we journey to our eternal home. According to **Job 22:28 (NKJV)**, "You will also declare a thing, and it will be established for you; so light will shine on your ways." This passage of scripture is a powerful reminder to the power of spoken words. From the scripture, we are taught that when we declare and decree according to God's Word, we are functioning in our authority and dominion, and we are activating our power! However, we must always be aware of the words we speak and the thoughts we think.

As Christians, our faith in God and His sovereignty gives us a safe place spiritually, mentally, and emotionally to address our fears. We use biblical affirmations to build us up when we feel the most torn down and when our faith is at its weakest point. Positive declarations are like concrete slabs or rocks on which a building or house is assembled. Positive words keep us focused, solid, and grounded on good and favorable things rather than on negative ones.

Speaking negative words is like constructing a house on quicksand; not only will the house be destroyed, but the inhabitants will be destroyed as well. In addition, when we speak negative words, we are creating feelings that will make us emotional and unstable. Biblical, positive affirmations empower us with stamina and strength to not quit, to not give up, and to keep moving forward in boldness, faith, and hope rather than in timidity and fear.

We are held accountable for every word we speak out of our mouths – "For by your words you will be justified, and by your words you will be condemned" **(Matthew 12:37, NKJV)**. As we decree the Word of God over our lives, we come into spiritual alignment with God's perfect will for us. The following are declarations we can speak in faith **(Proverbs 18:21, NKJV)** - "Death and life *are* in the power of the tongue, and those who love it will eat its fruit."

According to Holmes (2022), Everyday is declaration day! The most powerful claim of all is ***Jesus is Lord,*** states Holmes. As we declare that ***Jesus is Lord,*** forgiveness, identity, wisdom, acceptance, and salvation are released. We have a choice each and every day to decree and to insist on our future, so let's put these positive declarations into practice:

WHO I AM IN CHRIST...

I declare that I am **BLESSED**.
I am **DETERMINED**.
I am **ENCOURAGED**.
I choose to be **EXCITED**.
I choose to be **GRATEFUL**.
I am **MORE THAN A CONQUEROR**.
I choose to be **THANKFUL**.
I choose to be filled with **JOY**.

DECLARATIONS FOR MY CHILDREN...

I declare that my children will give me rest as I correct them.
I declare safety and ease for them day by day.
I declare that angels take charge, defend, and preserve them.
I declare that they are the head and not the tail.
I declare that they find favor and high esteem in Your sight.
I declare that they are teachable and obedient to Your will.
I declare that no harm shall come near their dwelling.
I declare that no weapon shall form against them.

DECLARATIONS FOR CHURCHES...

Declare a *FRESH* anointing in the sanctuary.
Declare souls are being saved from spiritual death.
Declare, Lord, that your message keeps on spreading.
Declare that people will receive the message with gladness.
Declare the Body of Christ become tenderhearted.
Declare that the Body of Christ forgives one another.
Declare that Your presence is with Your people with power.
Declare that the prayers uttered avail much.

DECLARATIONS FOR PASTORS...

Declare and confess that the Spirit of the Lord rest upon pastors.
Declare that the Gospel is preached to the meek, poor, wealthy, etc.

Declare binding up, healing the brokenhearted, and setting them free.
Declare that Your spirit will impart wisdom, power, and counsel.
Declare that Your spirit will manifest quick understanding.
Declare that the glory will rule, rest, and reside upon pastors.
Declare prosperity spiritually, physically, and financially.
Declare that the Gospel is preached boldly and courageously.

DECLARATIONS FOR HUSBAND AND WIFE...

We declare love to be shed boldly in hearts by the Holy Spirit.
We declare love is expressed and knitted together in truth.
We declare conduct is demonstrated honorably and of great price.
We declare that lives are lived in mutual harmony and accord.
We declare that each other is delighted, having the same mind.
We declare that hearts are kept in quietness and assurance.
We declare being heirs together because of the grace of God.
We declare this marriage is founded on Your word and love.

DECLARATIONS FOR FATHERS...

I declare that I will command my children and household.
I declare that I will keep the ways of the Lord.
I declare that I will do justice (living in honest relationships).
I declare that I will show judgment (making things right).
I declare that my faith is increased in order to please You.
I declare a ministry of reconciliation (bringing others to You).
I declare to see a GREAT move from You.
I declare to enter my position as a prayer warrior.

DECLARATIONS FOR MOTHERS...

I declare that I walk in love.
I declare that I speak ONLY words that build and edify.
I declare protection and care for my children.
I declare that I make the right decisions for my children.
I declare that Your Holy Spirit is poured upon my offspring.

I declare that I will correct and discipline them early.
I declare that I will teach them the Word of God.
I declare peace and undisturbed composure for my children.

DECLARATIONS FOR THE MOUTH...

I declare victory over my mouth by surrendering to God in prayer.
I declare discipline and control over my mouth through prayer.
I declare the power to restrain my mouth.
I declare to develop sensitivity over my words and conversations.
I declare a limit of my words when going through a storm.
I declare a guard over my lips.
I declare the words of my mouth are acceptable in Your sight.
I declare that I KEEP ON SAYING that Jesus is the solution.

DECLARATIONS FOR HEALING...

Declare that Your Word will not return void.
Declare that Your Word will accomplish what it says.
Declare that by Your stripes we are healed and made whole.
Declare that He sent His healing hand to rest upon me.
Declare Your life-giving powers flow into every cell of my body.
Declare Your healing hand cleanse, purify, and restore to wholeness.
Declare Your hand will heal and be strengthened for service.
Declare deliverance from death, harm, sickness, disease, etc.

DECLARATIONS FOR OUR CITY, STATE, NATION...

Declare and intercede for our mayors, governors, and president.
Declare and intercede for all who are in authority over us in any way.
Declare discretion for those in positions of authority.
Declare that your people dwell safely in this land and prosper.
Declare that the decisions of Your leaders are directed by You.
Declare that You cause leaders to lead quiet and peaceful lives.

Declare that Your people will humble themselves and pray.
Declare that blessed is the nation whose God is the Lord.

DECLARATIONS FOR PROSPERITY...

Declare that I do not want for anything.
Declare that I will walk uprightly before God.
Declare that I am the head and not the tail.
Declare that I am prosperous in life as my soul prospers.
Declare that all needs are supplied according to His riches.
Declare that as I give, it is given unto me.
Declare that as I tithe, windows of heaven are opened.
Declare blessings of the Lord make me rich and add no sorrow.

DECLARATIONS FOR PROTECTION...

I declare that You are my refuge and my fortress.
I declare that no evil shall be allowed to befall me.
I declare that You will cover me with Your wings.
I declare that no plague shall come near my dwelling.
I declare deliverance from the snare of the fowler.
I declare deliverance from deadly pestilence.
I declare that the adder, lion, and serpent are trampled under foot.
I declare a long and satisfying life.

PRAYER: Dear Lord, today we anticipate, decree, and proclaim biblical declarations as we speak forth Your promises to see real change in our lives. As we declare and decree Your Word, we are confident that You will perform what You told us You would do. We are assured of the hope that You will act, that You will do something, and that You are compassionately involved in our lives as we surrender ALL! In Your holy name. AMEN

2 ENCOURAGEMENT FOR THE JOURNEY

The following section is a compilation of brief daily encouragements.

TODAY'S ENCOURAGEMENT...

Colossians 3:17 (New Living Translation) "And whatever you do or say, do it as a representative of the Lord Jesus, giving thanks through him to God the Father."

This little verse sums up in a nutshell what the Christian's life should look like and how the born-again believer should behave moment by moment - in word and in deed, in mind and in motive. Let us remember that we are witnesses of His grace and His chosen representatives on earth. May all we do in word or deed be done in His name - giving praise and thanksgiving to God the Father, through Jesus Christ our Lord.

TODAY'S ENCOURAGEMENT...

We may not know what the future holds, but as we trust in the Lord and His sovereignty and His omniscience with all of our hearts, we can have peace and joy in the midst of the storms or trials. We have faith that God is directing our path, providing for our needs, protecting us, and ***CAUSING ALL*** things to work together for our ultimate good!!!

Romans 8:28 (New American Standard Bible)

"And we ***KNOW*** that God ***CAUSES*** all things to work together for good to those who love God, to those who are called according to His purpose."

TODAY'S ENCOURAGEMENT...

First Principle of the Gospel: ***FAITH***

Today I ask a question Jesus asked nearly 2,000 years ago: "...Nevertheless, when the Son of man cometh, shall he find ***FAITH*** on the earth?" **(Luke 18:8, KJV).**

Only when our faith is aligned with the will of our Heavenly Father are we empowered to RECEIVE the blessings we SEEK.

TODAY'S ENCOURAGEMENT...

Psalm 112:7 (English Standard Version) "He is not afraid of bad news; his heart is firm, trusting in the LORD."

Dear Lord, What hope we have in You as we can respond to bad news and not become fearful. We trust in You, O Lord, knowing that You are holding our hearts. Someone may be facing a crisis today, but they are not alone as we *LEARN* to lean on and to depend on You!!!

TODAY'S ENCOURAGEMENT...

We are admonished in **Isaiah 40:31 (KJV),** "But they that wait upon the Lord shall renew their strength; they shall mount up with wings as eagles; they shall run, and not be weary; and they shall walk, and not faint."

When we choose to wait on God, we are assured that what we are waiting for will *SURELY* come **(Hebrews 11:1)**. When we choose to depend on Him and *WAIT* for His timing, cooperating with Him and letting Him do according to His *WILL*, we will *NEVER* be disappointed!

TODAY'S ENCOURAGEMENT...(SHOUT NOW!)

Don't wait until the battle is over. Go ahead and *SHOUT RIGHT NOW!* Praise God in those valley moments. Praise Him *NOW* for the answers to prayers you are *EXPECTING* to come. Praise Him, believe in your heart that it is *ALREADY DONE* and watch God move on your behalf. *SUDDENLY*, you will see God manifest a *GREAT* change in your life. *SUDDENLY* you will see the mountain of problems being moved. *SUDDENLY* you will see those crooked places being made straight and the rough places being made smooth. *TRUST HIM, PRAISE HIM, BELIEVE HIM*, and **WATCH GOD DO IT!!!**

"About midnight Paul and Silas were praying and singing hymns to God, and the other prisoners were listening to them. *SUDDENLY* there was a violent earthquake, which shook the prison to its foundations. At once all the doors opened, and the chains fell off all the prisoners" **(Acts 16:25-26, NIV).**

TODAY'S ENCOURAGEMENT...

When we think about how SMALL we are and how GREAT God is, we should respond similarly to David who wrote, "Better is one day in your courts than a thousand elsewhere; I would rather be a doorkeeper in the house of my God than dwell in the tents of the wicked" **Psalm 84:10 (New International Version).**

A moment with God is better than an eternity without Him, and in His grace and mercy, we don't have to choose. By believing in Him, we can have an eternity with Him!!!

TODAY'S ENCOURAGEMENT...

Job 20:28 (NLT)

"You will succeed in whatever you choose to do, and light will shine on the road ahead of you."

Let us be mindful to **CONTINUOUSLY** choose and to continuously **DECLARE** to see God's grace, blessings, and favor manifested in our lives more and more!!! We must trust God with our whole heart and keep our expectation level on **HIGH** for the great things to come through unwavering **FAITH** and without doubt.

TODAY'S ENCOURAGEMENT...

"Beware that you do not forget the Lord your God..." **(Deuteronomy 8:11).**

Remember: The Israelites proved to be less faithful AFTER they moved into the Promised Land by turning their hearts to OTHER gods.

We MUST be aware of the temptation that success can bring. I once heard the saying, "There is no failure more disastrous than the success that leaves God out."

TODAY'S ENCOURAGEMENT...

Jeremiah 29:11 (New International Version)

"For I know the plans I have for you," declares the Lord, "plans to prosper you and not to harm you, plans to give you hope and a future."

God has the blueprint for our lives drawn up. He is guiding us and putting seeds in our hearts and, like a gardener, He waters the seeds He plants. God sees us, He hears us, and He answers our prayers. This life can be hard, but through trials, the Lord makes us stronger.

TODAY'S ENCOURAGEMENT...

The Prophet Isaiah exhorts us in **Isaiah 14:27 (Amplified Bible),** "For the LORD of hosts has decided and planned, and who can annul it? His hand is stretched out, and who can turn it back?"

When God gets ready to elevate you, ***NOTHING*** can stop what He has set into motion. All the forces of darkness cannot stop what God has ordained for your life.

TODAY'S ENCOURAGEMENT...

So often we underestimate the power of our prayers. Our prayers can go places we cannot go and accomplish things we cannot do on our own. The enemy knows just how powerful our prayers are and the power that we receive from God when we pray. That is the very reason why he works continuously to keep us distracted and disconnected from our power source. Let us always be mindful to make prayer a priority, not a last resort, and never stop praying!!!

"Pray without ceasing" (**1 Thessalonians 5:17, KJV**).

"The earnest prayer of a righteous person has great power and produces wonderful results" **(James 5:16b).**

TODAY'S ENCOURAGEMENT...

I don't know who needs to see this today, but **Isaiah 60:22 (ERV)** says, "When the time is right, I, the Lord, will come quickly. I will make these things happen." God is in control.

We may think that God's provision or response to our situation is too late, but it is not. He simply has His own timing, and it is us who need to adjust to His timetable, not the other way around. The question is, should we trust God's timing? Definitely, yes!

TODAY'S ENCOURAGEMENT...

Psalm 34:3 (International Standard Version)

"Magnify the LORD with me! Let us lift up his name together!"

Even though we all have problems, those problems don't have to have us. Just because a problem comes up, we don't have to keep our focus on it and continually talk about what's wrong. What we focus on magnifies and multiplies in our lives. Focusing on problems only breeds negativity and causes us to feel frustrated, aggravated, and irritated – and fills our mouths with complaints. But, focusing on God and our blessings in spite of the problems at hand breeds peace, joy, thanksgiving, and praise and increases our faith to provide the solution we need for any problem that comes up.

TODAY'S ENCOURAGEMENT...

Isaiah 41:10 (New International Version)

"So do not fear, for I am with you; do not be dismayed, for I am your God. I will strengthen you and help you; I will uphold you with my righteous right hand."

In this passage, God reminds us in comforting words that He will always be with us. He encourages us not to be FEARFUL as He will uphold us with His righteous right hand, allowing us to stand firm against ANY attacks of the devil!!!

TODAY'S ENCOURAGEMENT...

"You will keep in perfect peace all who trust in You, all whose thoughts are fixed on You!" **(Isaiah 26:3 - NLT).**

Through all of the chaos in our world today, PERFECT PEACE is the goal of humanity. The only way to achieve PERFECT PEACE that lasts into eternity is through total trust in God. Is God still on His throne, blessing and keeping His children? Then be steadfast (unmovable in your faith and trust in God). Has God sent His one and only Son to save us by His death on the cross? Then, we MUST trust in Him. He will never fail us. There is no other way. Then will come a steadfast (firmly fixed; unmovable) mind and **PERFECT PEACE!**

TODAY'S ENCOURAGEMENT… (FAVOR WITH GOD)

Proverbs 3:3-4 (NIV)

"Let love and faithfulness never leave you; bind them around your neck, write them on the tablet of your heart. Then you will win favor and a good name."

TODAY'S ENCOURAGEMENT… (THE SPLENDOR OF A KING, CLOTHED IN MAJESTY)

"Lord, Your name is so great and powerful! O LORD, our Lord, how majestic is Your name in all the earth, Who has displayed Your splendor above the heavens! People everywhere see Your splendor. Your glorious majesty streams from the heavens, filling the earth with the fame of Your name!" (**Psalm 8:1, NASB**).

PRAYER: Dear Lord, today the heavens declare Your glory, and earth unites with them in magnificent praise of Your holy name. You deserve our ceaseless worship and glory throughout time and into the eternal ages to come. Blessings and glory and wisdom and thanksgiving and honor and power and might be unto You for ever and ever. Amen.

TODAY'S ENCOURAGEMENT…

Psalm 91:7 (English Standard Version) "A thousand may fall at your side, ten thousand at your right hand, but it will not come near you."

TODAY'S ENCOURAGEMENT…

We would all prefer to avoid trouble, but affliction comes with a purpose. And even though it may not initially feel like it, that purpose is not to break us down but to build us up in our faith and trust in God. We have to stop letting the challenges we encounter work against us and start making them work FOR us, to DEVELOP our faith muscles, to STRENGTHEN our trust in God's ability to provide what we need, to make us BETTER, and to give us a testimony that will encourage and help others.

"For our present troubles are small and won't last very long. Yet they produce for us a glory that vastly outweighs them and will last forever" (**2 Corinthians 4:17, NIV**).

PRAYER: O God of all creation, open our spiritual eyes to see clearly that when troubles of any kind come our way, those are opportunities for great JOY!

TODAY'S ENCOURAGEMENT…

James 1:2 (NLT)

"Dear brothers and sisters, when troubles of any kind come your way, consider it an opportunity for great joy." God's face represents His presence. His face shining upon us speaks of His smile and the pleasure He takes in his people. …And Be Gracious to You. The result of God's pleasure is His grace toward us. We do not deserve His grace and mercy, but because of His love and faithfulness, we receive it!!!

TODAY'S ENCOURAGEMENT…

Acts 19:2 (King James Bible)

"He said unto them, 'Have ye received the Holy Ghost since ye believed?' And they said unto him, 'We have not so much as heard whether there be any Holy Ghost.'"

TODAY'S ENCOURAGEMENT…

"Look at how great a love the Father has given to us, that we should be called children of God. And indeed we are! The world doesn't know us because it didn't know Him" **(I John 3:1, Holman Christian Standard Bible).**

Someone has said that the truest proof of love is in giving.

PRAYER - Dear Heavenly Father, thank you for leaving Your heavenly home and coming to earth to give Your life as a sacrifice. And that's not how the story ends; three days later, You rose again! ***THAT'S LOVE — NO GREATER LOVE!!!***

TODAY'S ENCOURAGEMENT...

In Psalm 46:10 (ESV), God issues a command for all people to be still and to know that He is God. "Be still, and know that I am God. I will be exalted among the nations, I will be exalted in the earth!"

Stillness brings clarity (having a focused and clear state of mind). It draws one into the moment and makes thoughts and ideas clearer than they were before. Taking a simple moment to be still could be the difference between making a decision that will lead us down the wrong path and one that will lead us down the right one.

PRAYER: O Lord! Teach us to be still as we step away from the busyness of life and wait to hear directions from You! Help us to slow down for a few minutes and listen, truly listen, for Your voice. With Your help, we can learn to stay focused on Your vision for our lives, listen for Your direction and guidance, and allow You to calm our restless hearts. AMEN!

TODAY'S ENCOURAGEMENT...(LAW OF LOCATION)

Are you in the right location to be abundantly blessed by God?

"God took the man and put him in the Garden of Eden to work it" **Genesis 2:15 (NIV).**

God created the Garden of Eden, placed Adam in it, and told him to work. God said, "Be fruitful and multiply" **(Genesis 1:22 NIV).** In other words, "Be successful." However, there is a sequential order to receive ALL God has planned for us. *First:* God prepares a place for you. *Second:* He puts you in it. *Third:* He tells you to "work it." *Fourth:* He says, "I want you to succeed." That is called "the law of location." You only flourish in the place where you belong, doing what God has called and equipped you to do. And you'll have to work at it, so don't expect it to be quick and easy. The law of location is evident throughout the Scriptures.

PRAYER: Dear Lord, today enable us to get in our right place or location as we draw near to You and You will draw near to us. **(James 4:8 New King James Version)**

TODAY'S ENCOURAGEMENT

PRAYER: "A CALL for CALMNESS and PEACEFULNESS"

Dear Lord, grant me the serenity to accept the things I cannot change, the courage to change the things I can, and the wisdom to know the difference. AMEN!

Serenity: the state of being calm, peaceful, and untroubled.

The Serenity Prayer is a prayer written by the American theologian Reinhold Niebuhr (1892–1971).

TODAY'S ENCOURAGEMENT...

Dear Lord, if You were not the lifter of our heads, where would we be, where could we turn, or where could we go?

Psalm 3:3 (NKJV)

"But You, O LORD, are a shield for me, My glory and the One who lifts up my head."

TODAY'S ENCOURAGEMENT...(Thought-Provoking Questions)

What situation are you dealing with today that the enemy has convinced you God can not fix? Is there anything too hard for the Lord?

Jeremiah 32:17 (NIV) emphatically states, "Ah, Sovereign Lord, you have made the heavens and the earth by your great power and outstretched arm. Nothing is too hard for you."

TODAY'S ENCOURAGEMENT...

Proverbs 18:21 (NIV) puts it this way: "The tongue has the power of life and death." The stakes are high. Your words can either speak life, or your words can speak death. Our tongues can build others up, or they can tear them down. Today, we will choose to speak LIFE into our seemingly dead circumstances. In Jesus's name. AMEN!!!

TODAY'S ENCOURAGEMENT...

Psalm 46:1 (NIV) says, "God is our refuge and strength, a very present help in trouble." The reality is that there will be difficult times, but God promises to be our refuge (shelter from danger or trouble). When buildings crumble and our world is shaken by wars and rumors of wars, God has not failed us. He has promised to be with us in the middle of tragedy. FOR THIS we give God PRAISE - Hallelujah!!!

TODAY'S ENCOURAGEMENT...

How can Christians reduce STRESS?

Millions of people see their doctors every year for mental health issues, and stress is a leading cause. The most common causes of stress are money, careers, and relationships.

Stress is something that affects everybody from time to time. According to the American Academy of Family Physicians, stress can cause health problems such as high blood pressure, heart disease, and chronic migraines. There are healthy ways to deal with stress, and some are listed below.

1) Pray.

2) Go to bed on time.

3) Get up on time so you can start the day unrushed.

TODAY'S ENCOURAGEMENT...

1 Peter 5:6 (English Standard Version)

"Humble yourselves, therefore, under the mighty hand of God so that at the proper time He may exalt you."

The Bible teaches us to quit struggling and trust God will exalt us at the right time and place as He sees fit. He's a good Father who loves us; let Him be in charge of bringing us glory in due season!

As we willingly serve others, demonstrating ourselves as humble is not declaring that we are, in fact, insignificant. On the contrary, our humility in service to others is a declaration that our mighty God can be trusted to give us all the glory and recognition that we long for when the time is right!!! Let's be patient and wait on the proper timing of God to be exalted.

TODAY'S ENCOURAGEMENT...

Philippians 4:6 (New Living Translation)

"Don't worry about anything; instead, pray about everything. Tell God what you need, and thank him for all he has done."

PRAYER: Dear Father of ALL creation, I come before You to lay my panic and anxiety at Your feet. When I'm crushed by my fears and worries, remind me of Your power and Your grace. Fill me with Your peace as I trust in You and You alone.

TODAY'S ENCOURAGEMENT...

O Lord, my God, You are very great!!!

Psalm 104:1 (ESV)

The Psalm begins by considering the splendor of the heavens. The theme of this song of praise is the wisdom and power of God as seen in nature.

"Bless the Lord, O my soul! O Lord, my God, You are very great; You are clothed with splendor and majesty, Let all the Earth rejoice!"

TODAY'S ENCOURAGEMENT...

MOTHER'S DAY TRIBUTE (1)

Mother's Day gives people around the world the opportunity to shower the women who have loved and cared for them with honor and respect as taught in **Proverbs 31:26-28 (NIV)**: "She speaks with wisdom, and faithful instruction is on her tongue. She watches over the affairs of her household and does not eat the bread of idleness. Her children arise and call her blessed; her husband also, and he praises her."

PRAYER: O God, we especially pray for mothers who are stressed, mothers who are tired, and those who are grieving the loss of their mothers. I pray that You comfort all in the darkest hours of this weekend while so many others are rightfully celebrating. We ask You, Lord, to be the daily bread of single mothers who must lean solely on You for the fathering of their children.

We thank You that Your loving, outstretched arms will surround children who may never know their earthly fathers. We also pray for mothers who never had the honor of bearing children, but, through their nurturing, extend compassion to the many poor and needy whose lives they cross on our journey home!! Bless every mother and every grandmother with the finest of Your spiritual blessings! Amen! In Your name, Christ Jesus, we pray!

IF YOUR MOTHER IS STILL ALIVE, MAKE THIS DAY SPECIAL WITH HONOR AND RESPECT FOR HER. SOME OF US WISH WE HAD THE OPPORTUNITY TO HUG or CALL OUR MOTHERS! HOWEVER, we have the blessed HOPE that we WILL MEET AGAIN!

TODAY'S ENCOURAGEMENT...

MOTHER'S DAY TRIBUTE (2)

Mother's Day can bring a mix of emotions for many women. Let us remember those anticipating the birth of their first child, stepmoms wondering what their place is, those who have lost their mother and are faced with grieving on this Mother's Day, those who are moms who encounter feelings of hurt because their children have turned from God, and those overwhelmed with pain from the loss of a child.

On this day in which we honor mothers, may we love and cherish the special women who have given us birth, who have nurtured us, and who have prayed for our well-being.

PRAYER: Dear God of ALL creation, may our hearts overflow with gratitude to You, who formed and knitted each of us in a mother's womb. May You whisper deep within the spirits of mothers everywhere the sweet words she longs to hear from You—that nothing can ever separate her from Your love. Help her to nestle daily into the promises of Your Word, standing with faith on the things You declare are true. Let her know that You reward FAITHFULNESS and that TRUE SUCCESS does not lie in her accomplishments or accolades. Let her rest in the knowledge that she has done all she can, and that she and those she loves truly belong to You. Bless her with a servant spirit so she can teach her loved ones the joy of hearing one day, "WELL DONE!"

TODAY'S ENCOURAGEMENT…

FATHER'S DAY TRIBUTE
Proverbs 20:7 (Amplified Bible)

"The righteous man who walks in integrity and lives life in accord with his godly beliefs – How blessed, happy, and spiritually secure are his children after him who have his example to follow."

TODAY'S ENCOURAGEMENT…

Even though storms (both natural and physical) are inevitable in this life, I can remember the words my dear mother instilled in me as a young child - "Darling, storms don't last ALWAYS; they will pass!" However, while the storm is still raging in our lives, Jesus has assured us of many, many promises that will usher us into a subsiding storm.

Let's look at **Isaiah 41:13 (NKJV)**.

"For I, the Lord your God, will hold your right hand, saying to you, 'Fear not, I will help you.' " God promises to support and help us through every raging storm in our lives!

PRAYER: Dear Lord, today, whether someone has just emerged from a storm, is presently going through one, or about to enter one, thank You for so many promises given to us in Your word. Help us to rely wholeheartedly on these promises as we KNOW storms don't ALWAYS last! They will pass!

TODAY'S ENCOURAGEMENT…

What comfort and encouragement we have in the promises of **Isaiah 43:1-3 (NASB)**. "But now, thus says the LORD, your Creator, O Jacob, and He who formed you, O Israel, 'Do not fear, for I have redeemed you; I have called you by name; you are Mine! When you pass through the waters, I will be with you; And through the rivers, they will not overflow you. When you walk through the fire, you will not be scorched, Nor will the flame burn you. For I am the LORD your God, The Holy One of Israel, your Savior.' " These promises are to every Christian that God will be with us during our trying times and hard seasons.

The water, river, and fire represent afflictions, trials, and difficulties we face. But thanks be to God; He is with us in our most troubling times.

PRAYER: Loving Shepherd of the sheep, thank You for Your gracious promises, not only to Israel but to all of us who believe in Your name! AMEN.

TODAY'S ENCOURAGEMENT...

Can we have PEACE in the midst of a storm?

John 14:27 (NIV) reminds us, "Peace I leave with you; my peace I give you. I do not give to you as the world gives. Do not let your hearts be troubled and do not be afraid." So do not fear, for He is with you; do not be dismayed, for He is YOUR GOD!!!

Peace is not the subtraction of problems from life. Rather, peace is the addition of power to meet those problems; that power being the Holy Spirit and the promises of God.

PRAYER: Dear Lord, today help us to find peace in the midst of EVERY storm that life throws at us through Your holy spirit and Your faithful promises to us found in Your word!!!

TODAY'S ENCOURAGEMENT...

Psalm 145:18 (New International Version) "The Lord is near to all who call on him, to all who call on him in truth." When the peace of Christ rules in our hearts, thankfulness overflows. Even in the darkest of times, we can praise God for his love, his sovereignty, and his promise to be near us when we call.

PRAYER: Thank you, Lord, for Your peace that transcends understanding and Your love that endures forever.

TODAY'S ENCOURAGEMENT...

Matthew 5:3 (NIV) "Blessed are the poor in spirit, for theirs is the kingdom of heaven."

We are blessed when we are at the end of our rope, with less of us to depend on and more of God and His Kingdom to depend on. Also, our culture believes that we are blessed if we assert ourselves, are proud of ourselves, depend on ourselves, avenge ourselves, serve ourselves, or promote ourselves. On the contrary, we have to have help spiritually. We have to admit that we cannot survive on our own and that we need God to help us.

PRAYER - Dear Lord, help me to recognize my spiritual poverty and my need for You, Lord. I admit that I am spiritually broken and bankrupt, apart from You. Help me to become filled with You and less of me. Amen!!!

TODAY'S ENCOURAGEMENT...

Hebrews 4:16 (NIV) "Let us then approach God's throne of grace with confidence, so that we may receive mercy and find grace to help us in our time of need."

This is a verse that makes our hearts rejoice because, through Christ, we have received the gracious invitation to come boldly to God's throne of grace in our time of need. We should not come to the throne fearful, timid, or anxious. Rather, we are to come to Christ boldly, freely, constantly, ceaselessly, and persistently. WHAT AN AMAZING INVITATION AND HONOR!!!

PRAYER: Thank You, Father, for the grace and mercy that streams from Your throne of grace to me through Jesus Christ, my great High Priest and Heavenly Savior. I praise and thank You for the goodness and grace You have extended to me all of my life - even through the dreadful pandemic. I will FOREVER spend the rest of my days in grateful thanks and reverential praise as I express my love to You. Thank You. In Christ's name I pray. AMEN.

TODAY'S ENCOURAGEMENT...

The key to maintaining our FAITH is found in **Jude 1:24 (NLT)**.

"Now all glory to God, who is ABLE to keep you from falling away and will bring you with great joy into his glorious presence WITHOUT a single fault." Jude the Apostle taught us to remember that God is the One holding onto us and giving us the strength we need to remain true. That will help us to keep our focus on Him and the eternal hope that He offers to us.

PRAYER: Dear Lord, keep me from falling away and bring me ETERNALLY into Your presence faultless!!!

TODAY'S ENCOURAGEMENT - ANGELS WATCHING OVER US

Psalm 91:11-12 (NKJV) says He will command His angels to watch over us.

"For He shall give His angels charge over you, To keep you in all your ways. In their hands they shall bear you up, Lest you dash your foot against a stone." There's another world that we can't see with our natural eyes. If God were to pull back the curtain, we could see into that heavenly place. We could see all these forces that are for us. Powerful warring angels are at work on our behalf, standing guard, protecting us, pushing back the forces of darkness. We could see God moving the wrong people out of the way, placing the right people alongside of us to assist in the plan God has for our lives, lining up things in our favor, arranging good breaks, healing, and deliverance. Let us not get discouraged by what we see with our physical eyes.

Reminder, we are not doing life alone. In the unseen world right now, we are surrounded by powerful warring angels. We may be surrounded by trouble, but the good news is trouble is surrounded by our Most High God.

TODAY'S ENCOURAGEMENT...

Solomon warns us in Proverbs 20:22 (NLT), "Don't say, 'I will get even for this wrong.' Wait for the Lord to handle the matter."

This verse tells us not to think about repaying evil to anyone. We are exhorted not to take things into our own hands toward our offenders; rather we should let the LORD take care of them. Revenge comes from pride; a humble man does not worry about repaying evil. Revenge is blinding. It can easily lead to horrible crimes, including murder. Solomon's proverbs are about wisdom, and the blinding rage of revenge perverts one's ability to perceive, understand, and judge correctly. It destroys wisdom. And it leads to sinful actions. Faith in God is the only way to allow God to handle the matter because He will always take care of His own. This is wisdom and the will of God!!!

PRAYER: Dear Heavenly Father, extend great mercy and strength to not return evil for evil, to avoid the blinding dangers of grudges and revenge, so that You, Lord, will be allowed to repay vengeance bringing glory to Your name!!!

TODAY'S ENCOURAGEMENT...

Daniel 11:32 b (New King James Version)

"...But the people who know their God shall be strong, and carry out great exploits...."

(Exploits **- A deed or act; more especially, a heroic act; a deed of renown; a great or noble achievement)...**

The Bible declares a great promise in Daniel 11:32b, and this is one of the most courageous verses in the Bible. The Lord is looking for ordinary Christians through whom He can display His extraordinary nature. He wants to do mighty deeds that bear witness to the reality of who He is in us. God is raising up a people who will know Him intimately, who will be transformed into His image, and who will demonstrate mighty acts to manifest His power for the glory of His name.

PRAYER: Lord, use me to do exploits!!!

TODAY'S ENCOURAGEMENT...REPRESENTING JESUS

Colossians 3:17 (NIV) "And whatever you do, whether in word or deed, do it all in the name of the Lord Jesus, giving thanks to God the Father through him."

In this chapter, Paul gives clear instructions to Christians about living our faith in Christ. Since believers have been saved by Christ, they should not participate in the sins which trap unbelievers. For example, sexual immorality, jealousy, slander, revenge, gossip, etc., are not to be part of the Christian's life. Instead, believers ought to demonstrate compassion, humility, patience, and forgiveness. Above all, followers of Christ should show love. Paul also gives specific instructions for those living in Christian homes, including husbands, wives, and children.

PRAYER: Let my words and actions be acceptable in Thy site, O Lord.

TODAY'S ENCOURAGEMENT...

REMINDER: ...We are in a REALLY INTENSE spiritual warfare with our enemy Satan, and no one is exempt. Even children are being affected during these last and evil days!!!

A few of the most subtle devices Satan uses to win his battles are NEGATIVE self-talk, listening to the negativity of others or lies from our enemy, the devil. The best advice is to refrain from entertaining negative self talk, i.e., *I feel a headache coming on. I won't be able to pay my bills. I will never get out of debt. My children are so bad and I can't do anything with them. I believe I'm about to have a heart attack. I feel like I'm about to die.* Negative talk from others, or Satan, can do just as much damage, i.e., *You sure look bad today. What's wrong with you? You'll never amount to anything. It appears that you are gaining weight. When is your baby due?* On the contrary, DO NOT entertain negative talk from yourself or others.

In the HEAT of our spiritual warfare, my brothers and my sisters, it's OK to rest awhile – just don't quit!!!!!!!!!!!!!!!!!!!!!!!!!!!!!!!!!!

TODAY'S ENCOURAGEMENT...

Romans 8:28 (New American Standard Bible)

"And we know that God CAUSES all things to work together for good to those who love God, to those who are called according to His purpose."

The promise of Romans 8:28 that God works for our good "in all things" is reassuring; no matter the circumstances, God is CAUSING things to work in your favor. Today, take a moment to thank God for working all things together for your good, even in the circumstances where you can't yet see the result. Let us declare and decree: When I cannot see it, God, I still believe it. You are CAUSING all things to work together for my good!!!

TODAY'S ENCOURAGEMENT...

Galatians 6:2 (Amplified Bible) "Carry one another's burdens and in this way you will fulfill the requirements of the law of Christ." We are called to bear one another's burdens and to truly hurt along with those who are hurting. We care for one another as we demonstrate love for others with humility, gentleness, and patience. Our goal is to maintain peace and unity.

Supporting and loving others is so vital that Paul describes carrying each other's burdens as "fulfilling the law of Christ." It is this law which has inspired the church for centuries to show grace to those affected by issues of poverty and homelessness. When God lightens our burdens, let us do the same for others!

TODAY'S ENCOURAGEMENT...

Jeremiah 29:11 (New International Version) "'For I know the plans I have for you,' declares the Lord, 'plans to prosper you and not to harm you, plans to give you hope and a future.'"

As we live in tumultuous times, many Christians know and cling to Jeremiah 29:11 because it is helpful to remember that God has a plan for our lives, and this verse is a reminder of that. Christians facing difficult situations today can take comfort in knowing that Jeremiah 29:11 is not a promise to ALWAYS immediately rescue us from hardship or suffering, but rather a promise that God has a plan for our lives and regardless of our current situation, He can work through it to prosper us and give us a hope and a future!!

TODAY'S ENCOURAGEMENT...

Joshua 1:5 (New International Version) "No one will be able to stand against you all the days of your life. As I was with Moses, so I will be with you; I will never leave you nor forsake you."

This verse is an encouragement and an incredible promise from God. God originally gave this promise to Joshua when he led the people of Israel out of bondage in Egypt and into the Promised Land. But this promise is also given to ALL God's people as He continues to be with us in our triumphs and trials, fighting for us and rooting for us. Today, claim this promise personally!

TODAY'S ENCOURAGEMENT...

Romans 15:13 (NIV) "May the God of hope fill you with all joy and peace as you trust in him, so that you may overflow with hope by the power of the Holy Spirit." There is hope in God! According to the Bible, God is the God of hope. The word *hope* in the Bible is from the Greek word *elpis*. It means a DESIRE of some good with an EXPECTATION of obtaining it.

TODAY'S ENCOURAGEMENT...

Proverbs 16:24 (NLT) "Kind words are like honey—sweet to the soul and healthy for the body." This proverb tells us the wonderful value of speaking pleasant words to others. Kind words are grace-filled, gentle words that always seek to bring healing to others. As we speak kind words to others, our souls become healthy as well. In addition, dreams are set in motion and breakthroughs are accomplished when we speak positive affirmations to others.

Today, make a concerted effort to nourish someone's soul. Plan to live a life of saying kind words to bring healing to the soul and body of others, thereby being healed as well!!!

TODAY'S ENCOURAGEMENT...

Matthew 21:16 (KJV) "And [chief priests and scribes] said unto him, 'Hearest thou what these say?' And Jesus saith unto them, 'Yea; have ye never read, Out of the mouth of babes and sucklings thou hast perfected praise?'"

In Matthew 21:16, Jesus called it PERFECTED PRAISE – the key that silences the enemy. "Through the praise of children and infants you have established a stronghold against your enemies, to silence the foe and the avenger" **(Psalm 8:2)**. Small children can not always find the right words to say. Often their praise lacks depth because of their lack of communication skills and vocabulary. But their praise goes beyond being verbal.

Our praise may not always be very clear or even sound eloquent, but by the time it gets to the Lord's ears it has been **PERFECTED**. It is this praise that shuts the mouth of the enemy. Let us continue to offer up to God ***PERFECTED PRAISE!***

TODAY'S ENCOURAGEMENT...

TITUS 2:11-14 (ESV) "For the grace of God has appeared, bringing salvation for all people, training us to renounce ungodliness and worldly passions, and to live self-controlled, upright, and godly lives in the present age, waiting for our blessed hope, the appearing of the glory of our great God and Savior Jesus Christ, who gave Himself for us to redeem us from all lawlessness and to purify for Himself a people for His own possession who are zealous for good works!"

GRACE, which is AMAZING, is a gift from God that is offered to everyone FREELY, even a **WRETCH LIKE ME.**

TODAY'S ENCOURAGEMENT...

Psalm 145:3 (NLT), "Great is the LORD! He is most worthy of praise! No one can measure his greatness." GREAT ARE YOU, LORD!! One of the great anthems of the whole Bible, the Psalms in particular, declares His greatness which no one can fathom.

TODAY'S ENCOURAGEMENT...

May you be blessed with our Lord's love and peace on this day. **Psalm 3:3 (NIV),** "But you, Lord, are a shield around me, my glory, the One who lifts my head high."

You may be in a situation that is causing your head to fall. Fall because of weariness. Fall because of attacks against your life. Fall because the medical report is discouraging and hopeless. Fall because your finances may not be where they need to be. Fall because of situations on your job. On the contrary, don't stay focused on your circumstances or even deny the reality that the circumstances are REAL! Don't limit God. We serve a BIG God who is ALWAYS in control.

Therefore, lift up your head so the King of Glory may come in and turn your situation around! He's a way maker, miracle worker, promise keeper, light in the darkness, and the lifter of our heads.

TODAY'S ENCOURAGEMENT...

Wishing you all of God's blessings on this joyful day.

As children of God, our tongues have a lot of power. **Proverbs 18:21 (NIV)** confirms this by stating, "The tongue has the power of life and death, and those who love it will eat its fruit."

The stakes are high. Your words can either speak life, or your words can speak death. Our tongues can build others up, or they can tear them down.

I CHOOSE THE FRUIT OF LIFE!!!

TODAY'S ENCOURAGEMENT…

Lord, help us not to complain or worry when things don't go as we think they should. Help us to trust with all our heart that You are working things for our good. Help us to rise above disappointment and discouragement by shifting our thoughts away from the situation and giving thanks to You. Always keep us mindful to express our gratitude and give You praise for ALL that You have already done, for ALL that You are currently doing, and for ALL that You WILL DO in our lives!!!

Psalm 105:1 (NIV), "Give praise to the Lord, proclaim His name; make known among the nations what He has done."

TODAY'S ENCOURAGEMENT…WHAT A FRIEND WE HAVE IN JESUS!

Blessings, my friends!

Jesus gave everything to his friends—His knowledge of God and His own life. Jesus is our model for friendship because He loves us without limits, making it possible for us to live victoriously!

"God is my friend" is the first level of friendship with God, and we love the friendship of God. But the next level is when God says, "You are My friend." That is a great privilege!

TODAY'S ENCOURAGEMENT…

Mark 5:36 (NIV), "Overhearing what they said, Jesus told him, 'Don't be afraid; just believe.'"

Our faith is still required for God to work in us. Faith does not have to be big **(Luke 17:6, NIV)**, just pointed in the right direction **(Hebrews 11:6, NIV)** and persistent **(1 Thessalonians 5:17, NIV)**. It also needs to have the right intent. It is not biblical to have "faith" that God will give us riches or health **(James 4:2–3, NIV)**. Instead, God promises to give us what we need to do His will. If our hearts are aligned with His and we value what He prioritizes, we will be satisfied with what He gives us **(John 15:7, NIV)**.

It is okay to be disappointed when we don't receive the blessings we hope for if we also acknowledge that our hope ultimately rests in Him **(1 Peter 1:3, NIV).**

BELIEVING CAN STOP FEAR!!!!!!!!!!!

TODAY'S ENCOURAGEMENT…

Romans 8:15 (English Standard Version) "For you did not receive the spirit of slavery to fall back into FEAR, but you have received the Spirit of adoption as sons, by whom we cry, 'Abba! Father!' "

TODAY'S ENCOURAGEMENT - FAR MORE THAN MEETS THE EYE

II CORINTHIANS 4:16 (Christian Standard Bible) "Therefore, we never give up! Even though on the outside it often looks like things are falling apart on us, yet, on the inside we get new life day by day."

TODAY'S ENCOURAGEMENT…PASSIONATE PRAISE

Psalms. 28:7 (NIV), "The Lord is my strength and my shield; my heart trusts in him, and he helps me. My heart leaps for joy, and with my song I praise him."

TODAY'S ENCOURAGEMENT…

It's good to receive a word of encouragement from others, but sometimes you have to encourage YOURSELF!!! When you start to worship and praise God, worry begins to dissipate, so make the decision today that when worry comes your way, you will live **VICTORIOUSLY** and overcome worry with **PRAYER, PRAISE,** and **WORSHIP!**

And David was greatly distressed, for the people spoke of stoning him because the souls of all the people were grieved, every man for his sons and for his daughters. BUT David **ENCOURAGED HIMSELF IN THE LORD** his God, "And David was greatly distressed; for the people spake of stoning him, because the soul of all the people was grieved, every man for his sons and for his daughters: but David encouraged himself in the Lord his God" **(1 Samuel 30:6, KJV).**

3 POWER FILLED

John 16:7 (KJV), "Nevertheless I tell you the truth; It is expedient for you that I go away: for if I go not away, the Comforter will not come unto you; but if I depart, I will send Him unto you." One thing God is to us is our helper. Several times, God promised and described Himself as this. In Judaism, the Holy Spirit, also known as the Holy Ghost, is the divine force, quality, and influence of God over the universe and over His creatures.

This section will explain the power that comes with being filled with the Holy Spirit. Listed below are a few other names used to describe the Holy Spirit.

- Dove
- Holy Ghost
- Comforter
- Intercessor
- Paraclete
- Presence of God
- Spirit of Truth

I. **What is the Holy Spirit?**

- Christ in You, the Hope of Glory - **Colossians 1:27**
- If we do not have the Spirit of Christ, we are none of His - **Romans 8:9**

II. **How Do We Receive the Holy Spirit?**
- **A** - Admit we are sinners.
- **B** - Believe that Christ was born, He died, and He will return for a prepared people (*the Church - His Bride*).
- **C** - Confess our sins, and He is faithful and just to forgive us.

III. **Is the Baptism of the Holy Spirit for Children also?**
- Peter replied, "Repent and be baptized, every one of you, in the name of Jesus Christ for the forgiveness of your sins. And you will receive the gift of the Holy Spirit. The promise is for you and *your children*

and for all who are far off—for all whom the Lord our God will call" (**Acts 2:38-39, NIV**).
- "And afterward, I will pour out my Spirit on all people. Your ***sons and daughters*** will prophesy, your old men will dream dreams, your young men will see visions. Even on my servants, both men and women, I will pour out my Spirit in those days" (**Joel 2:28-29, NIV**).
- "No, this is what was spoken by the prophet Joel: 'In the last days, God says, I will pour out my Spirit on all people. Your ***sons and daughters*** will prophesy, your young men will see visions, your old men will dream dreams. Even on my servants, both men and women, I will pour out my Spirit in those days, and they will prophesy. I will show wonders in the heavens above and signs on the earth below, blood and fire and billows of smoke. The sun will be turned to darkness and the moon to blood before the coming of the great and glorious day of the Lord. And everyone who calls on the name of the Lord will be saved'" **Acts 2:16 - 21, NIV**).
- Jesus said, "Let the little children come to Me, and do not hinder them, for the kingdom of heaven belongs to such as these" (**Matthew 19:14 NIV**).
- "If you then, though you are evil, know how to give good gifts to your children, how much more will your Father in heaven give the Holy Spirit to those who ask Him?" (**Luke 11:13, NIV**).

IV. How Do We Walk in the Spirit?

- Walk in love - **Ephesians 5:2**
- Walk in Truth - **III John 1:4**
- Walk in Light - **I John 1:7**
- Walk in the Word - **Psalms 119:105**
- Walk in Wisdom - **Colossians 4:5**
- Walk in Faith - **II Corinthians 5:7**
- Walk in the Spirit - **Galatians 5:16**
- Walk in Name - **Micah 4:5**

V. How Can Music Create an Atmosphere for the Holy Spirit to Operate?

- Music can literally change the spiritual atmosphere in our homes, our cars, and in our places of worship.
- "And it came to pass, when the evil spirit from God was upon Saul, that David took a harp, and played with his hand: so Saul was refreshed, and was well, and the evil spirit departed from him" **(I Samuel 16:23, KJV).**
- Lucifer was created with pipes in his wings to worship God. **(Ezekiel 28:13 & 14)**
- David played his harp to drive depressed spirits from Saul.
- According to **II Chronicles 5:12-13,** when the singers and musicians praised God in song (there were over 120 priests playing trumpets alone), they all played "as one, to make one sound." That means that the musicians played with instruments, together in harmony. Also, the book of Psalms alone has 150 examples of songs that are recorded to show the right way to use music for praise.

Learning how to relax in the Lord through good, anointed, Christian music will really help take you out of yourself and all of your personal problems, while helping bring you back into God's presence, where His peace, love, and joy can be yours on a very regular basis!

PRAYER: Dear Lord, today, to our risen and soon coming King, we thank You for the gift of the Holy Spirit. We thank You for bringing us to turn from our sins to You for forgiveness, being baptized in Your name, and for dwelling in us by Your Spirit that we may be kept and preserved while journing in this present world on our way to our eternal home! In Jesus's name we pray. A

4 GIFTS OF THE HOLY SPIRIT

In providing for His church, God gave us gifts, not for our own uplifting but for building up the church. In **I Corinthians 12:7 (NIV)**, Paul taught the Corinthians about spiritual gifts. This is what he wrote. "To each is given the manifestation of the Spirit for the common good." In **1 Peter 4:10-11 (KJV)**, Peter emphasized this – "As each has received a gift, use it to serve one another, as good stewards of God's varied grace: whoever speaks, as one who speaks oracles of God; whoever serves, as one who serves by the strength that God supplies in order that in everything God may be glorified through Jesus Christ. To Him belong glory and dominion forever and ever. Amen."

God has not only created us because He wanted to, but He has also equipped us to advance according to His standards. Improving our own standards is not what God desires, but we should work for the betterment of others. Hence, this raises the question of how serving God shifts into serving others. When we serve God, we must know and obey His standards. God's standard of greatness is not the same as ours. For example, in **I Corinthians 13**, God's benchmark for love is putting others first. Therefore, we should put others first in order to follow His measure of greatness. In serving God, we will serve other people. So, in the Kingdom of God, we will use our gifts to serve others.

These gifts found in **I Corinthians 12** should ***NEVER*** be used to draw attention to ourselves or our ministry but be used as a sign pointing to Jesus Christ. When you discover your gifts, you will –

1) Understand yourself
2) Be released from guilt
3) Be released from an inferiority complex, and
4) Will discover your ministry

There are *nine gifts* of the Spirit which can be divided into three groups.

Inspirational Gifts (Utterance - to say something/vocal gift) - Prophecy, Gift of Tongues, and Interpretation of Tongues

Power Gifts (Do Something) - Gift of Faith, Working of Miracles, and Gifts of Healing

Revelation Gifts (Reveal Something) - Word of Wisdom, Words of

Knowledge, and Discerning of Spirits

Now, we will explore the nine gifts as they are divided into the three groups.

I. **Inspirational (Utterance - to say something/vocal gift) - Prophecy, Gift of Tongues, and Interpretation of Tongues**

   A. **What is Prophecy?**

   1. To declare that which could not be known by natural means
   2. Divine revelation of God
   3. To declare present and things to come
   4. Prophecy is given to the body or speaketh unto men for:

   - Edification (building up)
   - Exhortation (lift up, encourage)
   - Comfort (console)

   5. **Prophet (Seer)**

   - A spokesman for God
   - Interprets God's will

   6. **Prophets in the Old Testament were of two kinds:**

   Major Prophets (5)
   - Isaiah
   - Jeremiah
   - Lamentations
   - Ezekiel
   - Daniel

   Minor Prophets (12)
   - Hosea
   - Joel
   - Amos
   - Obadiah
   - Jonah
   - Micah

- Nahum
- Habakkuk
- Zephaniah
- Haggai
- Zechariah
- Malachi

B. **What is the Gift of Tongues?**

1. "Tongues" are the supernatural speaking of languages, never learned by the speaker; spoken as the Holy Spirit gives the ability to do so
2. When the body contacts the physical world
3. When the soul contacts the physical world
4. When the spirit contacts the spiritual world
5. The reason tongues are feared is due to a lack of understanding and resentment

C. Interpretation of Tongues

1. Not a translation, rather an interpretation
2. For example, in Daniel 5:25-28 (Mene, Mene, Tekel, Upharsin), "This is the inscription that was written: mene, mene, tekel, parsin. Here is what these words mean:
   - *Mene*: God has numbered the days of your reign and brought it to an end.
   - *Tekel*: You have been weighed on the scales and found wanting.
   - *eres*: Your kingdom is divided and given to the Medes and Persians."
   - Old Testament. the words that appeared on the wall during Belshazzar's Feast (Daniel 5:25), *interpreted* by Daniel to mean that God had doomed the kingdom of Belshazzar.

II. **Power Gifts (Do Something) - Gift of Faith, Working of Miracles, and Gifts of Healing**

A. What is the Gift of Faith?

1. Supernatural endowment by the Spirit whereby that which is uttered or is desired by man or spoken by God shall eventually come to pass
2. Substance of things hoped for and the evidence of things not seen

3. **Types of Faith**
    - Salvation Faith - Ephesians 2:8-9
    - Fruit of Faith - Galatians 5:22
    - Gift of Faith - I Corinthians 12
    - Strong in Faith- Romans 4:20

B. **Working of Miracles**
    1. Working of miracles is used to display God's power and magnificence.
    2. Miracles are compelling, staggering wonders, astonishment, or the working of an explosion of the Almighty.
    3. Miracles are divine interventions in the ordinary course of nature.
    4. By faith we receive the Word.
    5. Through faith we receive miracles and see the performance.
    6. God desires that we know the Word and put faith into action.
    7. Faith works closely to the working of miracles.
    8. By faith one can believe God in such a way that God honors the Word as His own and miraculously brings it to pass.
    9. By Faith, the sun stood still **(Josuah 10:12-13)**.

C. **Examples of Miracles (Faith in Action)**

    1. Dividing of the Red Sea
    2. Plagues in Egypt
    3. Moses threw down his rod and it turned into a snake.
    4. Axe head swimmed
    5. Hebrew boys in the fiery furnace
    6. Daniel in the lion's den

D. **Jesus worked in all nine Gifts**

    1. Worked in the five-fold ministry
    2. Disciple - learner of His Father

3. Servant as well as a friend
4. Jesus was a GREAT example

E. The purpose of miracles

1. To deliver God's people
2. To meet the needs of God's people
3. To do the work of God

F. To receive a Miracle

1. Invite Jesus into the situation.
2. Do not rush the Lord, but wait for a word from God.
3. **REMEMBER:** God is good, and He longs to give good things.

G. Gifts of Healing

1. Supernatural healing of diseases and sickness without any natural aid
2. The body is designed to heal itself in many cases.
3. Sicknesses
4. Begin to think healthy
5. Be in good health even as your soul prospers.
6. Let us speak the Word over our bodies, in the name of Jesus!
7. With His stripes we are healed. **(Isaiah 53:5)**
8. By whose stripes ye were healed? **(I Peter 2:24)**

D. Reasons to *NOT* receive healing

1. Many people do not feel worthy.
2. Others lack faith.

III. Revelation Gifts (Reveal Something) - Word of Wisdom, Words of Knowledge, and Discerning of Spirits

A. What is "Word of Wisdom"?

1. Revelation of the purpose of God concerning people, things, events in the future or looking to the future

2. Supernatural revelation of divine purpose and the will of God.
3. Knowledge - tells the problem
4. Wisdom - gives the solution
5. ***KNOWLEDGE WITHOUT WISDOM IS DANGEROUS AND VICE VERSA***

B. Word of Wisdom - Why is this gift referred to as "Word of Wisdom" instead of the **Gift of Wisdom**?

1. God does not give the entire or all of the ***words*** at one time - only "part" (***A Word***).
2. When a **gift** is given, it is given whole, and not in part.

C. Example of Wisdom
1. **Proverbs 15:1 (NIV)**, "A gentle answer turns away wrath, but a harsh word stirs up anger. The tongue of the wise commends knowledge, but the mouth of the fool gushes folly."
2. **James 1:5 (NIV)**, "If any of you lacks wisdom, you should ask God, who gives generously to all without finding fault, and it will be given to you."

D. Wisdom can be recognized by:

1. Dreams
2. Visions
3. Audible voice
4. Angels

E. If wisdom is not applied to knowledge, knowledge will be rejected.

5 MOUNT UP AS EAGLES

I have often wondered why God likens His children to eagles. He has a lot to say in His word about the eagle. In fact, the Bible mentions eagles over thirty times. Just what does God say and what does He want us to know about eagles? "But they that wait upon the LORD shall renew their strength; they shall mount up with wings as eagles; they shall run, and not be weary; and they shall walk, and not faint" **(Isaiah 40:31, KJV).**

This chapter examines the traits of an eagle to see why God wants us to have similar features. We will look at some awesome facts about eagles and see how they compare to the life of a believer. First, we will delve into exactly how they are able to fly (Bradley, 2021) and how they are able to soar without actually flapping their wings. Eagles' wings are built for soaring and gliding.

Eagles are born with big and heavy wings, with a wingspan between six feet and nine feet. For them, part of surviving is learning how to fly without actually flapping their big wings so they can conserve energy. Eagles can die if they exert too much energy flapping their wings during flight. As a result, eagles have to learn very early to wait for wind thermals (a big gust of wind that will rise up to them). Sometimes eagles will remain perched for days before they can catch a good, strong wind thermal and launch onto it. They combine flying and soaring on the wind to get them to where they want to go.

Just like the eagle has to learn how to catch the wind thermal in order to survive in this world, as Christians we have to learn how to be led by the Holy Spirit on a daily basis so we can fully accomplish everything God wants us to in this life (Bradley, 2021).

According to O'Chester (2021), eagles are the "king of birds" and throughout the Bible, God likens Himself and His children to an eagle. Eagles are considered an international symbol of authority, freedom, majesty, power, stamina, and strength. We cannot fly like an eagle unless we stay strong!

I believe God is trying to tell us something when He compares Christians to eagles. What does it mean "to mount up with wings as eagles"? I believe this means to put our trust in God and allow Him to lead our lives (Price, 1984). The eagle's safety lies in the sky. Our safety lies with our Creator, God. Bradley enlightens us on the traits eagles possess that Christians should have as well. A significant feature of eagles is that they are considered master ***fishermen***. They lock in on their prey and then swoop down to catch them. Just as eagles are known to be master fishermen when they catch fish in water, as Christians we are called by the Lord to be ***fishers of men***. Jesus called out to them, "Come, follow me, and I will show you how to fish for people"

(Matthew 4:19, NIV).

We must note here that even though eagles will mate for life, most of the time they are seen flying *alone* in the skies. As "Eagle Christians," many times we may feel totally alone, just as the eagle. The prophets of pre-Christian times differed widely, but one mark they had in common was their loneliness. They loved people and reveled in the religion of their fathers, but their loyalty to the God of Abraham, Isaac, and Jacob was of utmost importance, and that sometimes caused a feeling of loneliness. They realized that this world was not their home, as exemplified in **John 15:19 (ESV)**. "If you were of the world, the world would love you as its own; but because you are not of the world, but I chose you out of the world, therefore the world hates you."

Tozer (2016) informs us that there are two things remaining to be said concerning the Eagle Christian who may feel totally alone. First, the Eagle Christian who feels alone is not haughty, nor is he "holier-than-thou." Rather, he is likely to feel that he is the least of all men and is sure to blame himself for his loneliness. He wants to share his feelings with others and to open his heart to some like-minded soul who will understand him, but the spiritual climate around him does not encourage it, so he remains silent and tells his griefs to God alone.

The second thing is this: the Eagle Christian is not the withdrawn man who does not care about the suffering of humans and spends all of his time contemplating the heavens. Just the opposite is true. His loneliness makes him have sympathy for the broken-hearted, those who live in poverty, the fallen and the sin-bruised. Because he is detached from the world, as described earlier in **John 15:19 (ESV)**, he is willing and able to serve others (Tozer, 2016).

For the most part, eagles will be found living on some type of ***higher ground***. As Christians, because of who we are in Christ, we are already living on "higher ground" in comparison to the rest of the world. We are born-again children of the Most High God. We are now kings and priests of the Lord. The Holy Spirit, along with His power and knowledge, resides on the inside of us to help lead us, sanctify us, and empower us so we can all be used by the Lord in a mighty way as we serve others (Bradley, 2021).

Other very powerful traits of the eagle are being ***bold, courageous, and powerful***. Eagles have literally been seen fighting with poisonous snakes and tearing their heads off with their beak. They have been seen going right through major storm clouds where most birds would fly away and hide in safety until the storm has passed. So, as the eagle has no fear of any man, beast, storm, or snake, the Eagle Christian should have no fear of any demonic spirit or any evil human being since we all have God Himself totally on our side. "Behold, I give unto you power to tread on serpents and scorpions, and over all the power of the enemy: and nothing shall by any means hurt you" **(Luke 10:19, KJV).**

Due to the way eagles look and act, many people consider them *majestic and invincible.* They seem to have a look of royalty about them. In the same way, we have this air of royalty about us. We are considered kings and priests of the Lord due to the sacrifice that Jesus has personally made for all of us with His death on the cross. "But you are a chosen generation, a royal priesthood, a holy nation, His own special people, that you may proclaim the praises of Him who called you out of darkness into His marvelous light" **(I Peter 2:9, NKJV).**

The solitude of the eagle, his setting himself apart from all others, his freedom from natural forces such as gravity, and his swiftness all signify that the eagle is the most *majestic of all creature*s – and all these things are possible with man. One source of strength of the eagle is his diet: fish today, squirrel tomorrow, lamb the next day, etc. The Eagle Christian's source of strength is his diet which consists of attending church regularly, fellowshipping with others of like-precious faith, reading Christian literature, etc. The Eagle Christian has a great appetite, desiring daily living food **(I Corinthians 10:3-4).**

Another very interesting quality that eagles have is that they are very *patient.* Documentary film crews have filmed eagles spotting rabbits they target as prey. Once the rabbit senses the danger, he will go hiding in a hole, sometimes for as long as an hour or two, before he finally comes back out. The eagle will wait until the rabbit finally comes back out again. And once he does, the eagle will then swoop down and catch him within seconds. As a result of his patience, the eagle will then be rewarded with a big fat meal (Bradley, 2021).

In the same way, we all need the patience of the eagle, especially in the world of chaos that we are living in today. Everything is being done at an exponential speed, and the anger of many people is such that they will shoot to kill in minor disputes. "But if we hope for what we do not yet have, we wait for it patiently" **(Romans 8:25, NIV).**

Still another fascinating quality that eagles have is that they have *two sets of eyelids.* The first set is their natural eyelids which they use when they are in a resting mode. However, when they start to take flight on these strong wind thermals, they use a second set. This second set enables them to fly on these strong wind thermals without damaging their original eyelids.

As Christians, we also have two sets of eyes operating in us. The first set are our normal, natural eyes that we use to see the natural world in which we live. We also have a second set of eyes that are our spiritual eyes. When we have the Holy Spirit living on the inside of us, we also have His eyes available to us to see things from His perspective in the spiritual realm (O'Chester, 2021).

Many creatures that God created have ***color patterns*** that blend in with their natural surroundings to protect them from other predators. However, this is not true of the eagle. The American bald eagle has dark brown feathers with a white-colored head. Due to this contrasting color pattern, they can easily be seen from a distance. Just as the eagle, Christians who walk with an extremely powerful anointing from the Lord are especially noticeable from a distance. You can see the anointing of God all over them. You can see the manifest presence of the Holy Spirit in the form of a transparent glow radiating from their faces.

Eagle Christians have developed a specifically strong, personal relationship with the Lord. Therefore, over time, through prayer, and walking very close with Him, they are led by Him in their daily choices. Just like the eagle stands out in his environment as a result of his might, prowess, and contrasting color pattern in the animal kingdom, highly anointed Christians also stand out in their surroundings due to the presence and power of God Almighty Himself radiating through them (O'Chester, 2021).

Once you recognize all of the main qualities of the eagle, I do not think it is a coincidence that they all perfectly line up with what God would like to have worked into each one of us. I believe God wants us to resemble the eagle even as he likens Himself as an eagle: "God is like an eagle, in that He covers us and He shadows us **(Psalm 36:7, 63:7, 91:1-4, I Kings 8:7)**, covers us **(Psalm 91:1-4)**, hides us **(Psalm 17:8)** and is even under us **(Psalm 36:7)**."

Once again, here are the main attributes and qualities of the mighty eagle, the most powerful and feared bird in the skies.

- Master fishermen
- Flies alone
- Lives on higher ground
- Extremely bold, courageous, and powerful
- Majestic and invincible
- Very patient
- Has two sets of eyes
- Noticeable from a distance due to contrasting color patterns

God has raised the Eagle Christian up to be a heavenly creature, to be the head and not the tail, to know victory and not defeat. We must believe that we are MORE THAN conquerors! We must see ourselves as eagles who are majestic, strong, and FREE! **Isaiah 40:31** assures us, "They shall lift their wings and mount up (close to God) just as eagles." And **Proverbs 23:7** says, "For as a man thinks in his heart so is he."

    According to Price (1984), as an eaglet matures, he begins to resemble his parents more and more, and the same holds true with Eagle Christians. Let us examine ourselves today. Who do we look like? Are we ready to leave the ordinary behind? Do we *really believe* who we are as children of the Most High and that we serve a God who carries us and protects us with His feathers **(Psalm 91)**? It is obvious to see why God likens His spiritual children to the mighty eagle. Now is the time for God's people, all around the world, to rise above the clouds and crowds and mount up like eagles - ***alone!***

PRAYER - Dear Lord, We pray that we mount up with wings like the eagle **(Isaiah 40:31)** into the plan you have for our lives as promised in **Jeremiah 29:11**. Selah (So be it)

6 APPEAL TO PARENTS, GRANDPARENTS, AND FAMILIES

I encourage each of you – if you have influence on the next generation, or just know a child, youth, or teen – to make a concerted effort to inspire, to build up, to encourage, and to edify them as the enemy is turning the heat up. Just listen to or read current or breaking news daily. It could be someone in your family they are talking about next.

The MOST important job for adults is to teach children about Jesus. Ignorance of the scriptures causes one to error. Junior Bible Quiz (JBQ - 1st to 5th grades) and Teen Bible Quiz (TBQ - 6th to 12th grades) are tools used to plant the Word of God in our future generation, our next world changers, our global leaders, and our kingdom shakers. Those are only two tools (there are also many other methods) that can be used to prepare soldiers in the Army of the Lord and to equip them for the battles ahead. If we do not teach our children about the Word of God, they will not stand; when everything else passes away, the Word will still stand. As our children, youths, and teens encounter trouble, *and they will*, they will know how to run to God and not run to the world! JBQ and TBQ are not solely about learning scriptures or competing. They are also about learning tools to hide the Word of God in a young person's heart so WHEN the enemy comes, they will be able to speak like Jesus: "IT IS WRITTEN." **(Matthew 4:4). To God be the Glory!!!**

Invite EVERYONE to church, but especially our children, youths, and teens because there is an assignment from the pit of Hades to devour their lives.

PRAYER: O God, give me a heart of love and compassion to SNATCH some child, youth, or teen from the fire!

7 REWARDS AWAITING IN HEAVEN

I am so excited today as I begin to think about the heavenly rewards Christians will receive at the Bema Seat, or Judgment Seat, of Christ. The main reason for this enthusiasm is the fairness and justice that await us, unlike many endeavors in this earthly realm. If the athlete can successfully chase a perishable and temporary goal, how much more can we, as believers filled with the Holy Spirit, seek an eternal prize?

FIVE CROWNS

There are five heavenly crowns mentioned in the New Testament that will be awarded to believers. They are the ***Incorruptible Crown, the Crown of Rejoicing, the Crown of Righteousness, the Crown of Glory, and the Crown of Life.*** The Greek word for *crown* is *stephanos* (the source for the name Stephen, the martyr) and means "a badge of royalty, a prize in the public games, or a symbol of honor generally." Used during the ancient Greek games, it referred to a wreath or garland of leaves placed on a victor's head as a reward for winning an athletic contest. As such, this word is used figuratively in the New Testament of the rewards in Heaven God promises to those who are faithful (D'Ambrosio, 2020). Paul's passage in **1 Corinthians 9:24-25** best defines for us *how* these crowns are awarded.

Let us continue the discussion of crowns received by born-again Christians when at the judgment seat of Christ, given by Jesus Himself as described by D'Ambrosio (2020).

1) **The Incorruptible Crown – (1 Corinthians 9:24-25)**

I Corinthians 9:24-25 teaches us about the Incorruptible Crown that Christ will give for ***self-denial, self-control, and bringing our bodies into subjection to the Spirit*** - not allowing us to be slaves to our bodies. We have a choice of bringing our bodies into subjection so that we will be in control of every area of our lives: physical (eating healthy - bringing life to our bodies); mental (positive thoughts, guarding against depression, anxiety, worry and other mind-altering emotions); and spiritual (striving every day to abide in one of the prepared mansions made not by the hands of man). We all have the same opportunity to receive the Incorruptible Crown.

2) **The Crown of Rejoicing – (1 Thessalonians 2:19)** "For what is our hope, or joy, or crown of rejoicing? Is it not even you in the presence of our Lord Jesus Christ at His coming?" The apostle Paul tells us in Philippians 4:4 to **"rejoice always in the Lord"** for all the bountiful blessings our

gracious God has showered upon us. As Christians we have more in this life to rejoice about than anyone else. Luke tells us there is rejoicing even now in Heaven (**Luke 15:7**). The Crown of Rejoicing will be our reward where "God will wipe away every tear . . . there shall be no more death, nor sorrow, nor crying. There shall be no more pain, for the former things have passed away" (**Revelation 21:4**).

3) **The Crown of Righteousness – (2 Timothy 4:8)** "Finally, there is laid up for me the Crown of Righteousness, which the Lord, the righteous Judge, will give to me on that Day, and not to me only but also to all who have *loved His appearing.*" We inherit this crown through the righteousness of Christ which is what gives us a right to it, and without which it cannot be obtained. Because it is obtained and possessed in a righteous way, and not by force and deceit as earthly crowns sometimes are, it is an everlasting crown, promised to all who love the Lord and eagerly wait for His return. Through our enduring discouragements, persecutions, sufferings, or even death, we know assuredly our reward is being with Christ for eternity (**Philippians 3:20**). This crown is not for those who depend upon their own sense of righteousness or of their own works. Such an attitude breeds only arrogance and pride, not a longing, fervent desire to be with the Lord.

4) **The Crown of Glory – (1 Peter 5:4)** "And when the Chief Shepherd appears, you will receive the Crown of Glory that does not fade away." Though Peter is addressing the elders, we must also remember that the crown will be awarded to all those *who long for or love His appearance.* This word *glory* is an interesting word referring to the very nature of God and His actions. It entails His great splendor and brightness. Recall Stephen who, while being stoned to death, was able to look into the heavens and see the glory of God (**Acts 7:55-56**). This word also means that the praise and honor we bestow to God alone is due Him because of who He is (**Isaiah 42:8, 48:11; Galatians 1:5**). It also recognizes that believers are incredibly blessed to enter into the kingdom, into the very likeness of Christ Himself. As Paul so eloquently put it, "For I consider that the sufferings of this present time are not worthy to be compared with the glory which shall be revealed in us" (**Romans 8:18 NKJV**).

5) **The Crown of Life – (Revelation 2:10)** "Do not fear any of those things which you are about to suffer. Indeed, the devil is about to throw some of you into prison, that you may be tested, and you will have tribulation for ten days. Be faithful until death, and I will give you the Crown of Life." This crown is for all believers, but is especially dear to those who endure sufferings, who bravely confront persecution for Jesus, even to the point of death. In Scripture the word *life* is often used to show a relationship that is right with

God. It was Jesus who said, "I have come that they may have life and that they may have it more abundantly" **(John 10:10)**. Just as things such as air, food, and water are vital for our physical lives, Jesus provides us with what is required for our spiritual lives. He is the One who provides "living water." He is the "bread of life" **(John 4:10, 6:35)**. We know that our earthly lives will end. But we have the amazing promise that comes only to those who come to God through Jesus: "And this is the promise that He has promised us—eternal life" **(1 John 2:25)**. James tells us that this Crown of Life is for all those who love God **(James 1:12)**. The question then is how do we demonstrate our love for God? The apostle John answers this for us. "For this is the love of God, that we keep His commandments. And His commandments are not burdensome" **(1 John 5:3)**. As His children we must keep His commandments, obeying Him, ***always remaining faithful***. So, as we endure the inevitable trials, pains, heartaches, and tribulations—as long as we live—may we ever move forward, always "looking unto Jesus, the author and finisher of our faith" **(Hebrews 12:2)** and receive the Crown of Life that awaits us.

Remember: As born-again Christians, we have a promise – if we work, we will be rewarded! Today, let us become more aware of the significance of working hard in the kingdom so we may receive our crowns when rewards are issued to Christians at the Judgment Seat of Christ by Christ Himself. Selah (Think about it).

Philippians 3:13-14 (New International Version) "Brothers and sisters, I do not consider myself yet to have taken hold of it. But one thing I do: Forgetting what is behind and straining toward what is ahead, I press on toward the goal to win the prize for which God has called me heavenward in Christ Jesus."

The modern persecution of Christians worldwide is now more prevalent than any other time in history. Lives are threatened because people choose to follow Jesus. However, **James 1:12 (New International Version)** says, "Blessed is the one who perseveres under trial because, having stood the test, that person will receive the Crown of Life that the Lord has promised to those who love him." In addition to those who are persecuted for Christ, the Crown of Life will be given to all Christians who have exemplified patience in trials, a firm endurance, steadfastness, tenacity of purpose, and enthusiasm. Who, then, shall wear the Crown of Life?

Many feel that it is the responsibility of the local pastor, missionaries, etc., to win souls. But the Bible exhorts us in **Proverbs 11:30** that "he who wins souls is wise." We should be found winning souls at work, at school with friends, in the shopping malls, etc., telling them about the goodness of Jesus

EVERYWHERE we go!!! ("Letting your light shine before men so that God will get the glory" **Matthew 5:16.)** Remember: There is an eternal reward for doing so.

8 CONCLUSION

Tracks to Heaven 2 was designed to give a ***preparation perspective.*** We all must prepare ourselves to stand before Christ. ***Now*** is the time to prepare to meet Jesus. Many will stand before the Great White Throne, which is the place where God will bring judgment upon an unbelieving world **(Revelation 20:12-13, NIV).** On the other hand, only those who are born-again believers will stand before the Bema seat/Judgment Seat of Christ **(2 Corinthians 5:9-11)**. We believe, wholeheartedly, the scripture that states, "Behold, I am coming quickly! Hold fast what you have, that no one may take your crown" **(Revelation 3:11, NKJV)**. As we begin to have a ***preparation perspective*** of our eternal home, here ***are some questions we must answer. Are you preparing for that Holy City? Do you see Heaven in your view? Are you living your life in the light of His soon return? Are you ready?***

REFERENCES

Bradley, M. (2021). Traits of the Eagle and How It Pertains To Our Christian Walk.

D'Ambrosio, J. (2020). The 5 Crowns in Heaven. Retrieved from: https://www.soh.church/5-crowns-in-heaven.

Holmes, S. (2022). Declarations. Gateway Church-Shreveport, LA page 6.

O'Chester, H. (2021). The Eagle Christian: His Faith His Family His Foes Christian Faith Publishing, Inc.

Price, K. (1984). The Eagle Christian. Old Faithful Publishing Co.

Tozer, A. (2016). The Saint Must Walk Alone. https://www.worldinvisible.com/library/tozer/5j00.0010/5j00.0010.39.htm.

ABOUT THE AUTHOR

Dr. Norma Lee came from very humble beginnings. She was born and reared in Shreveport, which is ***north Louisiana's*** largest city and Louisiana's third most populous city. She grew up in the Stoner Hill neighborhood. Although she attended elementary school in the Lakeside neighborhood, she attended Central Free Methodist (a private school). There, she encountered her first study of the Bible. She and the other students had chapel each week and were urged to learn a Bible verse at each weekly gathering. The first Bible verse she ever learned was when she was in the 3rd grade – **Genesis 2:7 (KJV)**. "And the LORD God formed man of the dust of the ground, and breathed into his nostrils the breath of life; and man became a living soul." From that point on, the Word became a lamp to her feet and a light to her path **(Psalm 119:105, English Standard Version).** She attended Valencia High (Home of the Mighty Vikings) and graduated in 1970. She is a 1974 graduate of Southern University in Baton Rouge, Louisiana. She continued with her higher education at LSU-S and Centenary College. She received her Doctorate Degree in 2015 in Educational Leadership/Curriculum of Instruction from the University of Phoenix online program. Dr. Lee is an author of three books. Her most recent is titled ***Tracks to Heaven 2*** (this book). In 2019, she published her first book, ***Tracks to Heaven,*** and in March, 2022, her second book was published, ***Proven Strategies to Victorious Living.*** Currently, she is teaching in the Caddo Parish School System. She is also a member of Gateway Church-Shreveport, where Dr. J. Scott Holmes is Lead Pastor.

Made in the USA
Middletown, DE
21 December 2022